I CAN MAKE A DIFFERENCE

10 Ways I Can Earn Money

Sara Antill

PowerKiDS press.
New York

Published in 2012 by The Rosen Publishing Group, Inc.
29 East 21st Street, New York, NY 10010

First Edition

Editor: Jennifer Way
Book Design: Ashley Drago

Photo Credits: Cover Hill Street Studios/Getty Images; pp. 4–5 Jupiterimages/Liquidlibrary/Thinkstock; p. 6 © www.iStockphoto.com/Jim Jurica; p. 7 David Sacks/Getty Images; p. 8 © www.iStockphoto.com/ Morgan Lane Studios; p. 9 Joe Polillio/Getty Images; p. 10 © www.iStockphoto.com/Midwest Wilderness; p. 11 Jupiterimages/Creatas/Thinkstock; pp. 12–13 Jupiterimages/Brand X Pictures/Thinkstock; pp. 14–15 © www.iStockphoto.com/Goldmund Lukic; p. 16 Photos.com/Thinkstock; p. 17 © www.iStockphoto.com/ Galina Barskaya; pp. 18–19 iStockphoto/Thinkstock; pp. 20–21 Keith Brofsky/Stockbyte/Thinkstock; p. 22 Shutterstock.com.

Library of Congress Cataloging-in-Publication Data

Antill, Sara.
  10 ways I can earn money / by Sara Antill. — 1st ed.
      p. cm. — (I can make a difference)
  Includes index.
  ISBN 978-1-4488-6206-1 (library binding) — ISBN 978-1-4488-6371-6 (pbk.) —
ISBN 978-1-4488-6372-3 (6-pack)
  1. Money-making projects for children—Juvenile literature. 2. Success in business—Juvenile literature.
I. Title. II. Title: Ten ways I can earn money. III. Series.
  HF5392.A58 2012
  650.1'2083—dc23

                                          2011032484

Manufactured in the United States of America

CPSIA Compliance Information: Batch #WW12PK: For Further Information contact Rosen Publishing, New York, New York at 1-800-237-9932

Contents

Spending and Saving Money

Most of the things that we need in our everyday life cost money. Food, gas for the car, new clothes, and visits to the doctor all cost money. When you are a kid, your parents pay for most of these things for you. When you get older, though, it will be your **responsibility** to earn money and buy the things that you want and need.

In this book, you will read about 10 ways that you can start earning money now. Having money of your own, even if it is just a little, will help you practice smart spending and saving!

Raking leaves for your neighbors is a simple and fun thing you can do to earn money.

GARAGE
SALE
TODAY

Depending on where in the country you live and how your sale is set up, it might be called a garage, yard, stoop, or tag sale.

A **garage sale**, or yard sale, is a fun way to earn money. It is also a good way to get things out of your room that you no longer use. First, go through your old toys, books, and clothes. Decide what you would like to keep and what you would like to sell. Next, ask an adult to help you set up your sale and price your items. Put up flyers at school so everyone there knows about your sale!

On the morning of your garage sale, place all your items outside so people can start shopping. You can use a calculator to add up prices quickly.

2 Run a Lemonade Stand

A good place for a lemonade stand is somewhere lots of people walk by. Make sure you have permission to set up a stand before you start selling your drinks!

Many kids start lemonade stands to earn money. Lemonade does not cost a lot of money to make. All you need are lemons, water, sugar, and paper cups. People love to drink lemonade on hot summer days. Set up a table and make signs showing the price of each cup.

DELICIOUS CANDY APPLES

3 Hold a Bake Sale

If you like to bake, you could hold a bake sale. At bake sales, people sell baked goods such as brownies, cookies, and other treats. Wrap each dessert in its own individual package and price it. If you know other people who like to bake, each person can make a different treat and then keep the money from their sales.

Candy apples are another simple treat you can make and sell. Make sure an adult is there to help you when you are using the oven or other kitchen appliances.

Many people pay others to do yard work for them. See if any of your neighbors will pay you to rake their leaves in the fall. In the winter, you can offer to shovel snow from their driveways. You will earn money and get some exercise, too!

Shoveling snow is hard work, so people in your neighborhood might be glad to pay you to clear their walkways!

5 Have a Car Wash

Washing a car is a project you can do alone or with a group of people. See if your parents or neighbors will pay you to wash their cars. You and your friends could also hold a car wash for the whole neighborhood. Everyone can help, and then you can all split the money you earned!

School clubs often organize car washes because it is a simple way for a group of people to raise money.

6 Recycle!

Recycling is good for the Earth. When people recycle, it means that less trash goes into landfills. Did you know that as well as leaving your recycling out for collection, you can earn money by taking recycling to a recycling center?

The next time you drink from a glass or plastic bottle or metal can, look at the label. If you see the words "**refund**" or "value," that means the bottle can be returned to a recycling center for cash. Look on the Internet for a recycling center near you. You may get only 5¢ or 10¢ for each bottle. If you collect a lot of bottles, though, that money can add up fast!

Separate your refundable recycling from your recycling for collection until you have lots of refundables to take to the recycling center. You can do something good for the Earth and make money at the same time!

13

7 Be a Tutor

Do you get good grades in school? If so, you may be able to earn money as a **tutor**. Tutors work with other students one-on-one or in small groups to help them learn. You can tutor younger students or students in your class who may be having trouble.

Many tutors are paid by the hour. Decide how much you would like to charge for your time. Depending on the subject and number of students you will be working with, you can probably ask for around $5 or $10 an hour to start. Put up flyers at school to **advertise** your services!

If you have younger siblings, you can practice your tutoring skills by helping them with their homework. Good teaching skills will make you a valuable tutor.

15

8 Sell Your Crafts

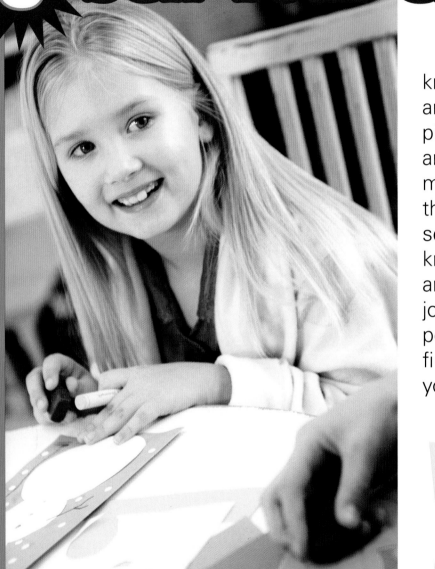

Some kids like to knit or **crochet**. Others are good at drawing pictures. If your crafts are well made, you may be able to sell them! You can start by selling to people you know. You can also ask an adult to help you join a Web site where people sell crafts or to find a craft fair where you can sell things.

Making greeting cards is a fun craft. You can make birthday cards, holiday cards, and other kinds of cards.

Knitting and crocheting are skills that take practice. Start by making simple items, and then make more challenging pieces as you become more experienced.

When you are selling something you have made, it is important to figure out the cost of the **materials** you used. Set the price higher than the cost so that you will earn a profit, or more than the cost of your materials.

Doing small jobs for your neighbors is a great way to earn money and help others. The best way to start is by letting people know that you are ready to work. Ask for your parents' permission to let your family's

friends or neighbors know that you would like to do jobs for them.

There are likely lots of jobs in your neighborhood. You could walk your neighbors' dogs after school, weed their gardens, or feed their cats while they are away. You can also offer to run **errands** or do household **chores** for people.

A neighbor might ask you to collect the mail while he or she is away. This is just one of many small jobs that your neighbors might appreciate that you could do.

10 Open a Savings Account

When you start earning money, you may want to spend it right away. However, it is important to learn to save some of your money for the future. Many people try to set aside 10 percent of their earnings. That would mean for every $10 you earn, you would save $1.

A parent or other adult will need to help you set up a savings account. A savings account can help you save up for something special.

A great way to save your money is by opening a **savings account**. A parent will need to help you set up the account at a bank. Savings accounts do not just help you save, though. They also help you earn money! Banks will pay you **interest** on the money in your savings account.

Earn Money Together!

Most of the moneymaking ideas in this book can be done on your own. Many of them, though, will be more fun if you do them with friends! Just make sure to keep a careful count of the money you earn so that it can be split fairly between everyone who helps out on a project!

Dog walking is a job that is fun to do with another person.

It is never too early to start learning how to earn money and spend it wisely. The ideas in this book are just the beginning. What other ways can you think of to earn money?

Glossary

advertise (AD-vur-tyz) To announce publicly, often to try to sell something.

chores (CHORZ) The household tasks that a person performs often.

crochet (kroh-SHAY) To tie thread in a special way with a curved needle.

errands (ER-undz) Small, everyday tasks done around town, such as going to the store or to the post office.

garage sale (guh-RAHZH SAYL) When people sell things they own but no longer want right outside their houses.

interest (IN-ter-est) The extra money that the bank pays someone with a savings account.

materials (muh-TEER-ee-ulz) What things are made of.

recycling (ree-SY-kling) Using things again instead of throwing them out.

refund (REE-fund) Money that is returned.

responsibility (rih-spon-sih-BIH-lih-tee) Something that a person must take care of or complete.

savings account (SAYV-ingz uh-KOWNT) A special place where a bank keeps money set aside for a person.

tutor (TOO-ter) Someone who teaches one student or a small group of students.

Index

B
bake sale(s), 9
bank(s), 20
bottle(s), 13

C
calculator, 7
car(s), 4, 11
chores, 19
clothes, 4, 6
crafts, 16

E
errands, 19

F
fair, 16
flyers, 7, 15
friends, 11, 19, 22

I
interest, 20

J
jobs, 18–19

N
neighbors, 10–11, 18–19

P
parent(s), 4, 11, 20
profit, 17

R
recycling, 12
responsibility, 4

S
savings
   account(s), 20
signs, 8
snow, 10
students, 14–15

Web Sites

Due to the changing nature of Internet links, PowerKids Press has developed an online list of Web sites related to the subject of this book. This site is updated regularly. Please use this link to access the list: www.powerkidslinks.com/diff/money/